IF I WERE Starting MY Ministry Again

JOHN M. DRESCHER

Abingdon Press/Nashville

IF I WERE STARTING MY MINISTRY AGAIN

Copyright © 1995 by Abingdon Press

All rights reserved.

No part of this work may be reproduced or transmitted in any form or by any means, electronic or mechanical, including photocopying and recording, or by any information or storage retrieval system, except as may be expressly permitted by the 1976 Copyright Act or in writing from the publisher. Requests for permission should be addressed to Abingdon Press, 201 Eighth Avenue South, P.O. Box 801, Nashville, TN 37202

This book is printed on acid-free, recycled paper.

Library of Congress Cataloging-in-Publication Data

Drescher, John M.

If I were starting my ministry again/ John M. Drescher.

p. cm.

ISBN 0-687-01001-2 (alk. paper)

1. Clergy—Office. 2. Pastoral theology. 3. Drescher, John M.
I. Title.
BV660.2.D74   1995
253—dc20

95-16812
CIP

Unless otherwise noted, Scripture quotations are from the New Revised Standard Version Bible, Copyright © 1989 by the Division of Christian Education of the National Council of the Churches of Christ in the USA. Used by permission.
Those noted KJV are from the King James Version of the Bible.
Those noted NIV® are from the HOLY BIBLE, NEW INTERNATIONAL VERSION®. Copyright © 1973, 1978, 1984. International Bible Society. Used by permission of Zondervan Publishing House. All rights reserved.
Those noted NKJV are from The New King James Version. Copyright © 1979, 1980, 1982, Thomas Nelson Inc., Publishers.

97 98 99 00 01 02 03 — 10 9 8 7 6 5 4

MANUFACTURED IN THE UNITED STATES OF AMERICA

*To the glory of God
and for the encouragement
of all those men and women,
called by God,
in the varied ministries
of the church of our Lord and
Savior Jesus Christ.*

≈ *If I Were Starting My Ministry Again . . .* ≈

I. I would seek to be more disciplined
in the cultivation of my own **spiritual life.**
13

II. I would seek to give much more time
to the **study and preaching** of Scripture.
25

III. I would seek to make my ministry more **Christ-centered.**
30

IV. I would try to remember that it is not my eloquence
but the **Holy Spirit's enablement**
which will accomplish Christ's purpose in my ministry.
36

V. I would seek to keep in mind that,
in spite of all its failures, **the church** is
the body of Christ doing God's work in the world.
42

VI. I would strive to lead and **equip**
each member for the work of ministering.
45

VII. I would look for and encourage **creative centers.**
51

VIII. I would place a primary emphasis on **prayer.**
53

IX. I would seek to always remember
that my calling is not to control people's faith
but to **love** them into the kingdom of God.

59

X. I would seek to always be aware
that God is at work, usually in persons, places, and programs
where I least expect God to be working.

64

XI. I would seek to always remember that I minister only out of overflow,
and that **fruit** is produced only on new growth.

68

XII. I would be strongly drawn to **church planting**
rather than to an established congregation.

73

≈ *Preface* ≈

For a number of years younger pastors particularly, as well as those in training for pastoring, urged me to write *If I Were Starting My Ministry Again*. No doubt this specific title was suggested because of my two former books, *If I Were Starting My Family Again* and *If We Were Starting Our Marriage Again*.

What follows has also grown out of my own search and need. Here are jottings on what seems important to me as I ponder where I would put the emphasis if I were starting my ministry again. They also touch on what I wish someone had shared with me when I began my ministry. Perhaps they were shared to a greater extent than I realize now. Many things do not register until one comes to relevant situations in life.

I have served as a pastor in three congregations, as bishop or overseer of congregations in three different conferences, and as a seminary teacher for a decade. I have also served as editor of a denominational weekly magazine for approximately 12 years. In addition it has been my privilege to speak in hundreds of congregations and ministers' groups which crossed denominational lines—Catholic and Protestant—and in such contacts ministers have asked the question, "What would you do if you were beginning again?"

From experience I know there are low points in ministry. After several years a minister may experience a dip which may test one's call and commitment. The excitement in entering the ministry may dissipate because we did not see the great growth we anticipated or we have not reached our goals. In middle age, as family comes on and other responsibilities weigh heavily, the minister is inclined to become discouraged or think of greener pastures. Middle age is a crisis when we again search for our identity and ask questions about the rest of life. It is a great time for a refresher course and a return to the basics.

William Nelson in *Ministry Formation for Effective Leadership* takes us back to some of these basics. "What is the impetus that motivated your Christian calling? What is the goal that presently guides your ministry formation? Is it a dedication to the study of the Bible, church history, or Christian theology in order to become a more effective teacher? Is it a passion to reform the structure that controls our society in order to make it possible for all persons to become truly human? Is it a desire to build up the body of Christ as a reconciling community of faith for the purpose of evangelizing the world? The critical capacity for self reflection will help you to articulate the goals you will set on the way to becoming an effective pastoral leader." [1]

Opportunities and joy given me in the Christian ministry have gone beyond all my expectations. Yes, as in all work, there have been the difficult times. But the Christian ministry, for me, was paced with challenges and was most fulfilling. No other calling touches every level of existence from birth to death. No other work feels more of life's deepest pains and life's highest joys. No other service shares more fully in people's failures and successes.

In spite of all the church's weaknesses and failures, it is still the one group in the world which demonstrates the most love, sacrifice, and caring. And even those who do not acknowledge Christ reap the blessings and benefits of the Christ-like spirit and impact.

Therefore, as one who has entered the fifth decade of ministry, I share some things which have proved a great blessing, some areas I would strengthen, and some ministries I would do differently each time I began again.

What I share is not proposed as the complete answer for every minister. Each minister must seek and find what God is saying, where one's own calling lies, and is given. One person cannot do everything, so each must, under God, be and do that which God calls one to and find those areas of strength and weakness, seeking God's blessing in both.

≈ I ≈

I would seek to be more disciplined in the cultivation of my own spiritual life.

"Jesus went up on a mountainside and called to him those he wanted, and they came to him. He appointed twelve—designating them apostles—*that they might be with him* and that he might send them out to preach and to have authority to drive out demons" (Mark 3:13-15).

This experience of being "with Christ" and practicing his presence for development of my inner life was not stressed enough throughout my theological train-

ing. I am thankful for those professors who left me with the impression that they had a deep devotional life, an intimacy with Christ which left me sensing they came from the presence of the Lord or had a prayer life so vibrant and vital that it carried into the classroom.

I entered the ministry with a clear sense of call and excitement to be in the ministry of Christ and the church. However, it took me some time to learn that fruit is only produced on new growth and that the Word I am to impart must first become flesh in me. It became clear that God needed to produce his work through me.

It did not take long in the pastorate for me to realize that I needed to nourish my own spiritual life. I needed to feed my own soul and to know the power which comes from being in the presence of Christ in his Word, in solitude, meditation, fasting, and prayers, if I was to do a spiritual and eternal work, and if I was to meet the deep hungers and cries of persons whom I met each day.

James N. McCutcheon points out that a glimpse into Jesus' private life "provides at least three impressions of our Lord's habitual practice that immediately speak to the minister's devotional life. He chose a time and place where he would likely not be disturbed. He did not permit even those closest to him to disturb his time in prayer. Yet his devotional life was always threatened and intruded upon by the needs around him."[2]

As we deepen our relationship with God it follows that our relationship with others will also be deepened.

David J. Bosch summarizes Lesslie Newbigin's contrasting of the "Pilgrim Progress Model" and the "Jonah Model" of the spiritual life. Pilgrim felt he needed to escape from the "wicked city." Jonah had to enter the city, with all its sin and corruption. Bosch concludes: "The two are absolutely indivisible. The involvement in this world should lead to a deepening of our relationship with and dependence upon God, and the deepening of this relationship should lead to increasing involvement in the world."[3]

In a real sense we need to be called out, separate from the world, before we can be sent into the world.

A young pastor wrote me, telling me that he had been perturbed and had publicly taken me to task some years ago in a ministers' conference because I put so much emphasis on the cultivation and discipline of the inner life. He felt we should get busy in the work of the church.

I did not remember the incident. Now, he confessed, after a few years in the ministry, he realized his inner emptiness and how essential it is to get to the source of spiritual strength and service. In cultivating his own spiritual life, a whole new spiritual world and work began to unfold before him.

Though verbal abilities, good management skills, and a pleasant preaching and visitation style may carry a minister for a while, soon one's moral integrity is at stake if one is speaking or seeking to minister beyond one's own spiritual depth or commitment.

The Abiding Life

In John 15 Jesus tells us twice that unless we abide in him and he abides in us we will accomplish nothing of spiritual or eternal worth. Nothing? The flesh still feels that it can through training, education, gifts, hard work, and other personal qualities do a spiritual work. Jesus says we cannot.

Unless we commit ourselves in daily openness to the Scripture, to meditation and prayer, we will be searching for our own spiritual identity in a short time. We will have less faith and confidence and we will have decreasing discernment of spiritual reality. Without daily abiding in Christ we become subject to the benumbing influence of the secular and the material, and we will give our time to secondary things—the machinery of organization, the church office, and running about the community, doing those things which can all be explained in natural terms.

Until we believe, with all our hearts, what Jesus said, "Apart from me you can do nothing," we will continue to function at the natural level, getting only what a natural, intelligent, educated self can produce. We will attend seminar after seminar to sharpen our skills but spend little time in solitude and prayer to have God shape our wills.

Time alone with God sharpens the focus of our priorities and opens us to receive God's presence and power. The intimacy of our lives with Christ is the measure of our spiritual power for God.

G. Byron Deshler in *For Preachers Only* writes: "It was at the close of a Sunday morning service in my first pastorate that a young layperson said to me, 'Byron, you must have spent some time with God this past week.' His remark shook me up. I had, in fact, spent much more time that past week in prayer and meditation than usual. It had not occurred to me that my people could detect whether or not I had spent time with God. If there was some quality in my preaching that indicated the sermon had evolved in communion with God, then the lack of this would also say something about my prayer life." [4]

"Be still, and know," says the Scripture—and there is a knowledge of God and God's work which comes only in communion with God until one senses the very breath of God on our lives and our labor.

What I speak of is not merely a technique or religious duty. It must be communion with Christ. God is one who "works for those who wait for him" (Isaiah 64:4).

Personal Priorities

In order to discipline myself I found it a great help to commit myself to certain clear priorities.

Priority One: I am committed to reading God's Word each day before I read anything else. Before I eat natural food it is pleasant to feed on the food for the soul and to satisfy the hunger for God and God's will. This priority has led me to rise early, to divide the New Testament into thirty parts so that it can be read in a month's time. This I do every other month and in the intervening month I read a sizable portion of the Old Testament. I need this discipline, and it has become as much a necessary part of life as eating the natural food each day.

Priority Two: I am committed to talking with God each day before I talk with anyone else. In addition to this being a time of praise and thanksgiving where I seek to meditate on God's character and his gifts, I find that a prayer list is helpful for me. Some prayers, petitions, or persons on the prayer list are long-term and some are short-term. There are those for whom I have prayed every day for many years. There are others named in prayer for shorter and specific lengths of time.

Some persons have raised the question, What happens, if, for some reason, I need to answer a telephone call or speak to someone before my early morning reading and prayer time? My response is that this, in no way, breaks my commitment. One makes a commitment to be on the job each workday at a certain time. When some emergency comes along we do not say, "The commitment is broken so I guess it's no need for me to go to work on time regularly again." Neither does an emergency or interruption, which has happened very seldom over the years, cause me to give up this commitment to reading the Scripture and prayer.

Closely connected to these first priorities has been journaling. Journaling, although not necessarily a daily exercise, has been vital as I express my meditative thoughts, my prayers, and longing in written form.

Priority Three: I am committed to fasting at least one meal a week and periodically for more lengthy times. Jesus says "when you pray" and "when you give," assuming that his followers will pray and will give. He does not modify it to "if you fast." He says "when you fast," assuming his followers will fast. John Wesley would not ordain a minister who did not fast at least two days a week, and he points out that it was assumed all Methodists fasted each week. Every time of spiritual renewal involves also a renewal in the practice of fasting.

Fasting for spiritual purpose gives me a greater sense of dependency upon God for all of life and ministry, a greater sensitivity to the Holy Spirit and the Word, and greater awareness of God's presence and blessing in all of life. It is also a great help in dealing with temptations of the flesh and spirit.

Dallas Willard writes in *The Spirit of the Disciplines,* "This discipline teaches us a lot about ourselves very quickly. It will certainly prove humiliating to us, as it reveals to us how much of our peace depends upon the pleasures of eating. It may also bring to mind how we are using food pleasure to assuage the discomforts caused in our bodies by faithless and unwise living and attitudes—lack of self-worth, meaningless work, purposeless existence, or lack of rest or exercise. If nothing else, though, it will certainly demonstrate how powerful and clever our body is in getting its own way against our strongest resolves."[5]

Priority Four: I seek to read a chapter from some worthy book each day, beyond the required or usual reading for sermon preparation and other church work. I seek to read books varying between the older classics and more recent books. I seldom read a best-seller the first year, but, if a book is a best-seller the second and third year, it is probably worth my time.

"Making wise choices about what you read is an act of responsible stewardship," says Thomas R. Swears. "A helpful guideline for such decision making is to maintain a balanced reading program. Such a balance helps keep the pastor from becoming too narrowly focused in counseling, teaching, or preaching images. Images guiding a pastor's thinking and speaking ought to have enough diversity to enable a pastor to respond appropriately to a wide variety of human needs."[6]

Yes, if I were starting my ministry again I would start here—the deepening of my own spiritual life through the above spiritual disciplines as first priorities. I wish someone had suggested such an approach at the beginning of my ministry.

"Who Do People Say I Am?"

Leslie Weatherhead of England was once scheduled to speak to a group of Manhattan ministers. His ship was delayed by the fog and the ministers waited for a number of hours. When Dr. Weatherhead arrived he said, "You have waited a long time and I have come a long way to ask you one simple question, Do you know Jesus Christ?"

At first glance this may seem like a strange question to ask a group of ministers. Yet here is where we must start if we would minister for Christ. Here is what our people are waiting to know. And those to whom we minister are able to sense if we know Jesus personally and if we came from his presence.

The first of seven statements to shepherds in the book of Jeremiah is the complaint, "The priests did not say, 'Where is the LORD?' Those who handle the law did not know me" (Jeremiah 2:8). The result is that the people committed two evils: they forsook the Lord, the fountain of living water, and they dug out cisterns for themselves, cracked cisterns that could hold no water (Jeremiah 2:13).

First Things First

Before the giving of a commission there must be the companionship.

We must learn to know Christ before we can preach Christ.

We must commune before we can communicate.

We must be ministered to before we can minister.

We must be disciplined before we can discipline.

We must love our Lord before we can labor for the Lord.

We must adore Christ before we can adorn his doctrine.

We must see God's glory before we can speak of God's glory.

We must wait for the vision before we can share the vision.

We must tarry before we can teach.

We must worship before we can do spiritual work.

We must seek Christ before we can share Christ.

We must abide in Christ before we can produce abiding fruit.

We must practice Christ's presence before we can preach his person.

We must meditate before we can mediate.

The secret of effective service is seeking Christ in secret.

Then we will hear his whisper above the words of the world.

Then we will hear his call above the cries of the crowd.

Then we will feel his touch above the touch of criticism.

Then we will know God's love above the love of self and things.

Then we will know God's power above the power of the evil one.

Then we will hear God's message above the mumblings of the world's message.

Then we will see Christ's Lordship above our own position, prestige, or pleasure.

Then we will live a life which cannot be described in natural terms.

Discipline for Renewal

Finally, in the words of Suzanne Johnson, "The question to be put to any practice of spiritual discipline is the question of *adequacy*. Spiritual disciplines authenticate the Christian life when they invoke compassion in us, sensitize us to what God is doing in the world, prompt us to embrace the stranger, inspire in us heartfelt affection for God and neighbor, create in us the capacity for self-giving love, and lead us to authentic self-love. If a spiritual discipline does not open us to the qualities of character, we likely are practicing a bogus spirituality."[7]

I am certain that many frustrations pastors feel come from a lack of discipline. Not only can regular devotional life and serious Bible study easily go by the wayside, but days can be frittered away fiddling on the insignificant and the little nothings.

Without a pattern and discipline of meditation and prayer, study, sermon preparation, visitation, and relaxation the minister will accomplish little and become shallow and sluggish.

I would remind myself continually that, when the Scripture speaks about the minister's calling it compares its discipline to the unrelenting practice of an athlete (I Timothy 4:6-10), the unentangled commitment that a soldier makes (II Timothy 2:1-7), and the unashamed and faithful servant of Christ (II Corinthians 2:14-19).

"Does God have favorites?" asked a frustrated minister of an aged bishop.

"No!" replied the bishop, "But he does have intimates."

≈ *II* ≈

I would seek to give much more time to the study and preaching of Scripture.

The second statement about God's desire for the shepherds of God's people in Jeremiah is that God wants to give them shepherds after God's own heart, who will feed them with knowledge and understanding (Jeremiah 3:15).

The Scripture's command to the minister is to "preach the Word" (II Timothy 4:2 NIV). The early disciples gave themselves to "prayer and the ministry of the Word" (Acts 6:4 NIV).

It should be obvious that to preach the Word the study of Scripture is primary. I would seek to get intense training in the biblical studies. Dwight L. Grubbs in *Beginnings—Spiritual Formation for Leaders* writes, "The dignity of a vocation is always to be measured by the seriousness of the preparation made for it."[8]

I would select carefully a school where there is a strong biblical studies program, and emphasis on spirituality and preaching of the Scripture, and an unmistakable practical evangelistic fervor. Teachers who have had a profound reverence for the Scripture, a contagious spiritual life, and a Christ-centered message have had a powerful impact on my own life.

When Alexander Maclaren was approached to become pastor of the church in Manchester, England, he asked, "Do you want my feet or my head? I cannot give you both." If they wanted his feet to do all the chores and run all the errands and attend all the committees, they should not expect him to preach sermons or teach the Bible with any depth. The congregation told Maclaren it wanted him to be faithful in the call of God to "preach the Word." And so he did.

Common Escapes

One of the escapes from the serious study of Scripture is to become enmeshed in boards, committees, meetings, and organizations in church and community. The charge to "preach the Word" is disobeyed, and the ordained minister becomes devoted to the muchness and manyness of the machinery of the church and community, to the detriment of one's own spiritual growth, spiritual ministry, and life of the church. The charge to minister is not to build an organizational empire but to exalt Christ. It is to make full proof of the ministry of the gospel. It is not to run an office but to reach persons with the offer of grace and salvation.

This means I would give a great deal of time to teach my people the great cardinal truths of the Scripture. Only as persons are grounded in the Scripture can they grow in faith, for "faith comes by hearing and hearing by the word of God" (Romans 10-17 NKJV). We are not told to pray for faith. We can have no more faith in God or in Christ than we know about him. Therefore I would seek to enlarge my people's understanding of God, of Christ, of the Holy Spirit, and all the cardinal doctrines of the faith. I would preach more expository messages, leading my people through book after book of the Bible. A temptation is to take a text and preach from it, sometimes rather far. The Lord has not promised to bless my word but he has promised to bless God's Word.

Time is needed to study the Bible. This means I would avoid committees like the plague. I would let those who have the gift of administration take care of such as much as possible. Perhaps more than any other one thing, ministers get bogged down and blamed for all kinds of failure because of their turning from the preaching and teaching of the Word to the running of the organization.

In days when the weather severely limited travel, pastors would "winter" with a subject, author, or a book of the Bible. This meant that the minister would set aside hours each day, for six or more months, to make a particular study of a book of the Bible or of a biblical doctrine or subject.

If I were starting my ministry again I would winter each year with one book of the Bible, or a series of short books such as I, II, and III John, reading, listening to the Spirit through meditation and prayer, learning what others have said about such a passage, and learning all I could about this particular book. In twenty years or less I could, in this way, become profoundly versed in all the New Testament books, plus other books of Scripture.

I would also winter with great writers. A wonderful way to learn to know intimately the great persons of the ages is to read all such persons have written and to ponder why such continue to speak. To take a period of priority time each day to read all the writings of any great theologian or writer would surely be life-changing and maturing.

Primary Focus

Every vocation has its primary focus along with related tasks. A teacher teaches, a physician doctors, a carpenter builds, and a painter paints. A true minister of the gospel preaches and teaches the Scripture. Preaching is the primary function of the ordained minister.

One of the failures of today's minister is the loss of the passion for preaching and teaching. Too many succumb to the "jack-of-all-trades" job description instead of demanding of themselves and the congregation the commitment to preaching required by the minister of Christ, made clear in the first call and charge as a minister.

Specifically the preaching task requires hours of uninterrupted meditation upon the Bible passage integral to the sermon, translation, study of commentaries, reading, and the careful preparation of outlines.

A congregation will learn to respect a minister's schedule of sermon preparation if valued enough by the preacher. If I were starting my ministry again I would subordinate all other tasks to the original call and charge "Preach the Word."

God has planned that "through the foolishness of preaching" (I Corinthians 1:21 NKJV), persons are saved, changed, freed from the old self and from sinful habits to serve the living Christ in full freedom of faith.

≈ *III* ≈

I would seek to make my ministry more Christ-centered.

It is very easy to become issue-centered or problem-centered. It is also easy to be caught up in all kinds of questions without ever arriving at Christ who is the answer.

Scripture is to lead us to Christ. We need to strive, in all our preaching, to do the same. "For no one can lay any foundation other than the one that has been laid; that foundation is Jesus Christ" (I Corinthians 3:11). Paul also writes "May I never boast of anything except the cross of our Lord Jesus Christ, by

which the world has been crucified to me and, I to the world" (Galatians 6:14).

We need to do all we are able to help people see, hear, and respond to Jesus Christ in conversion, commitment, and service. We are not his disciples until we follow him completely ourselves and until we help others to become his disciples.

This means primarily reconciliation to God through the incarnation, cross, and resurrection of Christ. It means leading persons to Christ's saving grace and to live and witness for Christ in every place and situation. It means leading persons in surrender to the Holy Spirit who longs to reveal Christ to us, to reveal Christ in us, and to reveal Christ through us.

Many years ago a missionary shared with me that he found whenever the death and resurrection of Christ was preached, the Spirit of God was active in bringing salvation to persons. The gospel is "the power of God unto salvation to all who believe." No wonder Paul wrote, "God forbid that I should glory, save in the cross of Jesus Christ" (Galatians 6:14 KJV). When we preach Christ, in his finished work of salvation, the energy of the Holy Spirit is released and lives are changed, freed from the old life, from sinful habits, and from the bondage of sin. There are interesting sermons. But the power to change lives is missing when Christ and his cross are missing.

A big part of our problem is that, particularly for a second generation church or preacher, we preach and teach the effects of the gospel rather than the gospel itself. So the Holy Spirit cannot use our message to bring conviction and conversion. Taking up the cross is understood clearly only after one has been saved by the cross.

Nels Ferre became a well-known theologian in America. Ferre was born in

Sweden and at the age of 13 left home to come to America. The departure was unforgettable. That morning the family had prayer. Each of eight children prayed. When they had finished, they walked to the station together. Ferre said, "I could see Mother, her mouth forming words, and not saying anything. Finally, the conductor blew his whistle and the train began to pull away. Mother half ran along the platform, and finally overcoming her emotion in the trauma of that awesome moment, the last words I heard her say were these, 'Nels, remember Jesus.'"

Paul, writing to the preacher Timothy says, "Remember Jesus Christ" (II Timothy 2:8).

Christianity Is Christ

Christian preaching is preaching Christ. Much preaching is about Christ. If I were starting my ministry again I would determine to preach Christ in every sermon.

Preaching Christ should include at least five specific areas. First I would present him as a living presence, as one who is distinct from a historical figure of the past. Jesus is alive. He is the risen glorified Savior and Lord. This is why Christ's resurrection is so central. This means I would remind my hearers that Christ is present in the gathering of believers. "Go and preach" says Jesus, "and, lo, I am with you always" (Matthew 28:20 NKJV).

To preach Christ means also that I would seek to represent myself as Christ's ambassador, bringing a message from the living Lord. I speak his ideas, his words, and his message and not my own. This means I would present the claims of Christ upon my hearers: "Behold! The Lamb of God who takes away the sin of the world" (John 1:29 NKJV).

To preach Christ means also to present him as a present deliverer from the power of sin. It is to believe, as Oswald Chambers wrote: "Yielding to Jesus will break every form of bondage in any human life."

It is even possible to testify to Christ's work in our lives in such a way that we point to ourselves rather than to Christ.

To preach Christ means to preach his teachings. If Jesus is Lord and Master then the master's message is to us. It is the message we must also proclaim. And that message, found in the Gospels, speaks not only about our beliefs but also about our behavior.

E. Stanley Jones in *The Christ of the Mount* writes painful yet powerful and much-needed words. "As the Apostles' Creed now stands you can accept every word of it and leave the essential self untouched. . . . We have locked up this ideal of Christ [The Sermon on the Mount] in high towers of reverence and respect. We have gone off to fight the battle of life in our own way, on our own principles, or lack of them—to our own disaster."[9]

But, to be faithful, we dare not lock Jesus' teachings in some ivory tower or relegate them to a future era, when enemies or other adversaries, with whom we are to relate in Christ-like ways, will be absent. To preach Christ is to preach and teach the central, timeless teachings Christ gave specifically to his disciples.

Beware of Cultishness

To preach Christ further I would seek to attract and invite persons to Christ not myself, or to a certain heritage or other unifying doctrine or "unique truth."

Eldon Trueblood in *Signs of Hope* discusses the rise of personality cults. He points out certain dangers and warns particularly of the greatest danger of all.

"This is the danger, which comes so easily in connection with strong and attractive personalities. Some otherwise wonderful movements in the modern world are deeply spoiled by the willingness of leaders or organizers to receive adulation from followers. Cultishness is always bad. *The one certain test that a movement has become a cult lies in the presence or absence of disciples of the group leader.* If a man welcomes or even permits personal disciples he is always suspect. Only One who ever lived was good enough to have disciples. More religious leaders are ruined by the flattery of admirers than by another single factor. The real cure is a double one: a devotion to Christ so genuine that a man sees himself in his right size, and a lively sense of humor."[10]

The above could be written regarding any religious leader such as a professor or teacher, as well as a preacher. The danger is even more pronounced in an age when advertising is designed to market celebrities, so that their fans can be tapped for further merchandise. When someone seeks to unite people around oneself rather than around Christ, it is a cult. The tendency can also apply to denominations. When the effort is to unite people around a common heritage or a peculiar doctrine rather than around Christ, it is also a cult. I would unashamedly preach and teach the uniqueness of Christ for salvation and commitment to him as Lord of all of life. This means to believe that there is no other name given under heaven whereby we shall be saved.

If I have learned one thing from a careful study of great spiritual awakenings in the past, it is that Christ is presented and the unity around him overshadowed every other difference or peculiar doctrine and practice.

Either we believe the unique message of the gospel of Christ or we do not. I for one want to say, "On Christ the solid rock I stand—all other ground is sinking sand."

If I were beginning my ministry again I would seek to affirm the centrality of Jesus Christ for salvation and his lordship for all of life. Without this there is no Good News to proclaim.

≈ *IV* ≈

***I would try to remember that it is not my eloquence
but the Holy Spirit's enablement which will accomplish
Christ's purpose in my ministry.***

All the blessings God has for us are made a reality by the Holy Spirit.

"And his strength is shown in my weakness." Most of us are too strong for God to use us. As long as we feel that we can do a spiritual or eternal work ourselves the Lord will let us keep trying. But the result will only be human.

This means that I must believe that the smallest seed planted and watered by the Spirit can bring forth abundant harvest, while the deed or word motivated by self will lie dormant and worthless as far as a spiritual work is concerned. God does not require success but faithfulness.

John Milton, frustrated in this blindness, came to believe:

God does not need
Either man's works or his own gifts.

Who best
Bear his mild yoke, they serve him best.

The mild yoke is to do what falls to us to do, trusting God to bless and multiply.

This means also that we should not feel that we are either a success or a failure simply by how skillful or how inadequate a service or sermon seemed to be. I've learned that it was not the sermons I felt were my best that God used. It was often the sermons and the service in which I felt inadequate or even a failure that God picked up and used for blessing.

This, of course, does not say we should not do our best in preparation and presentation of our message. What it does say is that we do not do God's work in the arm of the flesh but when we realize "all is vain except the Spirit," that is, unless the Holy Spirit energizes our message or service with power and conviction.

The Gospel Has Power

I would pay more attention to the inner voice which arises out of prayer and solitude.

I agree with Henri Nouwen in *Making All Things New,* "The more we train ourselves to spend time with God and alone, the more we will discover that God is with us at all times and in all places."[11] Though some may not have found this true, for me, to obey the inner voice to visit someone, to speak a word of comfort or warning, to make a contact has proved to be the leading of the Holy Spirit.

I well remember the urge to visit a man some distance from the church. He was a man I did not know well. I was hesitant. But, obeying the inner voice, I found him home from work, and working in his small garden. I also found him ready to accept Christ. He urged me to speak to his wife and later she also came to know Jesus, and they were baptized together.

To listen to the inner voice in changing an illustration in a sermon or even an entire message has proved the leading of the Holy Spirit, the One who knows the need of each person present. And although some word or illustration was used of the Lord in one setting, that does not automatically mean that God will use it in another. This calls for complete and constant dependence on the leading of the Holy Spirit.

Not Merely Intellectual

We make a great mistake when we imagine that spiritual truth can be understood by intellectual or rational means. It is wrong to believe that Bible study itself can remove the veil which keeps us from spiritual perception. The Scripture does not say, "No one knoweth the things of God except one studies the Bible." It tells us that "no one comprehends what is truly God's except the Spirit of God" (I Corinthians 2:11).

It is possible to grow up in the church, know all the doctrine, be fanatically faithful and yet not know God at all or understand spiritual truth. Put it down that we are spiritually blind to the things of God without the Holy Spirit's illumination. "Those who are unspiritual do not receive the gifts of God's Spirit, for they are . . . unable to understand them because they are spiritually discerned" (I Corinthians 2:14).

Great persons, mighty in intellectual, emotional, and volitional powers, are always present. And such may seek after God and seek to interpret spiritual truth.

But it is not correct psychology, oratory, overpowering logic, dynamic personality, or willpower which will convert or correct persons to the truth. "The world did not know God through wisdom" (I Corinthians 1:21). Paul says, "My speech and my proclamation were not with plausible words of wisdom, but with a demonstration of the Spirit and of power" (I Corinthians 2:4). Soul culture or intellectual power cannot open spiritual eyes.

"If you have to be reasoned into Christianity, some wise fellow can reason you out of it! But when the Holy Spirit brings inner illumination, no one can reason you out of it" (A. W. Tozer).

Cause of Emptiness

A primary cause of emptiness in many a sermon, Sunday school class, or Bible study is not that correct facts are absent. It is because it is not more than an intellectual discussion from a rational viewpoint—hence, there is no spiritual illumination. Of course, there must be knowledge of the facts. This is why the Bible stresses our need to know. But until there is illumination of the Holy Spirit nothing happens. Many can testify that after years in the church and hearing many sermons in many Bible classes, suddenly they receive a love, a longing for, and an understanding of Christ and his Word which cannot be understood aside from Holy Spirit work.

Am I against the discipline of the mind? No, but before we make spiritual progress we will need to admit that we cannot by our own intellect understand spiritual things. No amount of intellectual reasoning could have persuaded Paul that Christ was the Savior of the world. No amount of intellectual persuasion would have brought Peter to the conviction of all present, "God has made this Jesus, whom you crucified, both Lord and Christ" (Acts 2:36 NIV). He knew it only by the Spirit of God. And without the Spirit we can go on repeating the Gospel stories and facts, even in dramatic and scholarly form, yet leave hearts empty of spiritual refreshment, insight, and strength.

One has a strong feeling that much which is called irrelevant in preaching and teaching today is not poor preaching or teaching. What makes the message hollow is that the Holy Spirit is not present to give life and meaning. Why? Because we think that we can somehow do a spiritual work ourselves, because we do not pray for Holy Spirit illumination. Because we do not recognize our need of the Holy Spirit and covet his work. God is thus unable to bestow gifts and a blessing of spiritual illumination to us. God cannot lead us into all truth because we do not long and look for the Spirit to lead us.

Praise God that persons of all ages are growing tired of what the flesh can do, and that they are not satisfied with the husks of human reasoning and intellect! And thank God, many, in confessing their own inadequacy and opening themselves to the Holy Spirit of God, have found new freedom and power in living and witness. When this happens Christ becomes precious and his power is present. Greater are a few simple words from a believer who knows the touch of the Spirit than great words from one who feels that one's own wisdom or power will perform spiritual work. Do we really believe the saying that, "all is vain except the Spirit" does the work and bears God witness?

≈ *V* ≈

I would seek to keep in mind that, in spite of all its failures, the church is the body of Christ doing God's work in the world.

The church will always be the most successful mission in the world. Jesus said that strongholds of hell will not stop it. This persuasion takes away the pessimism so often found in the pulpit. It also does away with the feeling that the success of the church depends on us alone.

As with all precious relationships, so also with the church, there is at times a love/hate relationship. Because we care deeply we are many times deeply disappointed, even ashamed, to be part of a group which professes so much and practices so little. It is good then to remind myself of my own frailties and faithlessness and that I would never wish to be judged by my worst moments. Neither should I judge the church or any member by its worst performers.

Many times, I confess, I have felt like Carlo Carretto.

How baffling you are, O church,
and yet how I love you!
How you have made me suffer,
and yet how much I owe you!
I should like to see you destroyed,
and yet I need your presence.
You have given me so much scandal—
yet you have made me understand
sanctity.
I have seen nothing in the world more
devoted to obscurity, more compro-
mised, more false, and I have
touched nothing more pure, more
generous, more beautiful.
How often I have wanted to shut the
doors of my soul in your face and how
often I have prayed to die in the
safety of your arms.
No, I cannot free myself from you,
because I am you, although not
completely.
And where should I go?[12]

God Is Faithful

I would seek to remind myself that
Christ is always raising up his faithful
ones. And if in one area of the world the
church fails to respond to the Holy Spirit
and in obedience to his word, he will find
his faithful ones elsewhere. So I need to
avoid a narrow view of the church and see
that Christ is at work throughout the
world, that his cause will not fail or be
discouraged.

I would remind myself, especially when I feel lonely in my task or position, that God has faithful people. I would remind myself of God's word to Elijah when he said to the Lord, "I alone am left, and they are seeking my life, to take it away." Then the LORD said to him, " 'Go, return on your way . . . I will leave seven thousand in Israel, all the knees that have not bowed to Baal, and every mouth that has not kissed him' " (I Kings 19:14-18).

Elizabeth O'Connor writes, "We are not called primarily to create new structures for the church in this age, we are not called primarily to a program of service, or to dream dreams or visions. We are called first of all to belong to Jesus Christ as Savior and Lord, and to keep our lives warmed at the hearth of his life. It is there the fire will be lit which will create new structures and programs of service that will draw others into the church to discern and have vision."[13]

≈ *VI* ≈

I would strive to lead and equip each member for the work of ministering.

One of the most essential tasks and responsibilities of a pastor is to equip and enable each member to minister. Each Christian has received a gift. Each should be encouraged in every way to use that gift for kingdom work. A pastor who is not enabling members for ministry is finally a failure, no matter how great a preacher, organizer, or promoter of church programs such may be.

Ephesians 4:12-16 is one passage which points out this primary function of a spiri-tual leader. It is "to equip the saints for the work of ministry, for building up the body of Christ, until all of us come to the unity of the faith and of the knowledge of the Son of God, to maturity, to the measure of the full stature of Christ. We must no longer be children, tossed to and fro and blown about by every wind of doctrine, by people's trickery, by their craftiness in deceitful scheming. But speaking the truth in love, we must grow up in every way into him who is the head, into Christ, from whom the whole body, joined and knit together by every ligament with which it is equipped, as each part is working properly, promotes the body's growth in building itself up in love."

This beautiful passage gives clear guidance as to the final aim of all our preaching, teaching, and service. All our work is to equip each member to not only grow into the likeness of Christ and to have spiritual discernment but to fulfill each person's place in the building of unity, growth, and love in the body of Christ. Our task is to encourage, edify, and enable each member in the body of Christ so that each will sense the significance of Christ's call and assume the responsibility to use one's gift for the building up of the body of Christ.

The Final Test

Here is a kind of final test of the effectiveness of one's ministry. Some have built great followings through their eloquence and dynamic personality or speaking ability. Large congregations have grown up for a generation around such leaders. The test, however, is when these strong personalities go off the scene. The test is whether they were the equippers of others to minister. Many times such leaders have had only a following of admirers but have not produced a body of believers who are ministering doing Christ's work in the world.

I remember a prominent preacher of a prestigious congregation lamenting this very fact. He pointed out that the congregation was built around one well-known preacher. After this minister's passing the congregation searched for another preacher who could command the same kind of following. Now he was one in such a succession of ministers. His lament was that the congregation, over the years, was a gathering of sitters rather than servers. The people loved to listen but they had never learned to labor for the Lord. The congregation was like a group of individuals who came to be entertained at a theater rather than a body, knit together, equipped and working together for the building of itself in love.

Like many ministers, I began with the assumption that the work of the church was my responsibility. But what a challenge and relief when I saw that my call was to equip each believer to live the life of Christ and to do the work of Christ in the world right where each one lived! Today I'd rather be the pastor of a dozen people who are being equipped and active in all kinds of service than to be the pastor of a thousand people who fill the pews but who have little idea of what it means to function as Christ's body. At least Christ must have thought this was the way to go about that work. He is our example and leads the way in discipling persons for ministry.

The Great Commission

In the Great Commission (Matthew 28:18-20) the command is to make disciples. The other three participles "to go," "to baptize," and "to teach" are for the discipling ministry. Some observers point out that the decline of the church in Western Europe was due to a lack of discipling over the years. The North American church is heading in the same direction today.

In *The Disciple-Making Pastor,* the best recent book on discipling persons that I am aware of, Bill Hull tells us that not much will change for the good in the church, until pastors begin training disciples as Jesus did. Until congregations allow pastors to spend their time on training the spiritually well minority, rather than serving the unmotivated and disobedient majority, people will not live and serve as Christ intends.[14]

If I were starting my ministry again I would devote preparation, time, and individualized attention to discipling persons who in turn could disciple others.

An inadequate discipling ministry is evident when it is difficult to find persons to fill teaching and serving positions in the congregation, when Bible study and prayer groups cease to grow, when giving is on a plateau, when there is not ardent concern for the non-churched and world missions, and when a *congregation* does not produce ministers and spiritual leaders equivalent to its own need and beyond.

Central to pastoral leadership is a discipling laity with spiritual gifts which are discerned, developed, and deployed. If this kind of discipling is not happening, I would consider starting my ministry again.

At one point in my ministry I designed a discipleship course and invited any interested persons to join me for an extended period of study and practical experience. I wanted to begin with only those who felt the urge to join in this kind of course. However, only a few persons expressed an interest at all. So the idea was dropped.

I now see that Jesus *selected* and *called* certain persons to enter his training program, after prayer and fasting. Therefore, if I were starting my ministry again, I would design a course and select and call 10 or 12 persons in the congregation, inviting them to join me in this extended and serious discipling course. One of the goals of such a study is that when the course is finished the new disciples of Jesus would then become teachers of another group. In this way the discipling could greatly expand the body of Christ.

It is apparent that the Sunday school, preaching, and other congregational programs are not doing the job of discipling persons. A better way must be found. It is impossible to improve on the method of Jesus, and if I were starting my ministry again, I would make this kind of discipling a major responsibility of my ministry.

≈ *VII* ≈

I would look for and encourage creative centers.

While traveling one day I began reading a business magazine. One article caught my attention. The writer said that any business which finds its creative center and goes with it will prosper. Immediately numerous creative centers in the congregation came to my mind. In every congregation there are those persons who have particular interest in prayer and fasting. Each congregation has others who have special interest in the study of the Scripture, in stewardship, teaching, hospitality, in different kinds of service and mission, outreach, in music, in family concerns and counseling, in youth, older adults, singles, health concerns, and numerous other areas of interest.

A leader who will encourage the interests of persons and enable persons in these areas of interest, will have a rich reward. To wait until everyone or a large part of the membership has the vision before encouraging persons in the particular interest, means that many ideas or projects will be stifled or never begun.

So if I had it to do over again, I'd pay special attention to those creative centers, and I would do all I could to encourage persons who express interest or show particular concern or vision in one area or another. I believe God gives these gifts to the church for the benefit of the entire body, and often the best things which happen are those which begin with the interest or vision of one or two persons. If I would find such a creative center I would go with it and believe that the church will prosper.

Too much of my time in ministry has been spent with persons who have no desire to grow, to minister, or to be nurtured. I think I would have been much further ahead if I had encouraged those who had a desire to grow and serve and then given these persons opportunities to share what God is doing in their lives. One young person on fire for Christ can stir a whole youth group. One father or mother, faithful to Christ, can stimulate every family. One person of prayer can be used by God to turn the tide of spiritual lethargy. Such persons need the encouraging word and they will likely do more in the renewal of spiritual life than many, many sermons.

≈ VIII ≈

I would place a primary emphasis on prayer.

In God's third statement to shepherds in Jeremiah, God says that the results of lack of prayer on the part of leaders are stupidity and sluggishness. They have no message, they do not prosper, and the sheep are scattered (Jeremiah 10:21).

Always before God does a work among his people it is preceded by prayer on the part of his people. Every spiritual awakening begins as a movement of united prayer. Knowing this to be true, and as one who has studied and taken great interest in the history of spiritual awakening down through the centuries, I would seek to lead my congregation in becoming a people of prayer. Prayer had a primary place in the life of our Lord. He was an example of prayer, and he urged his disciples to pray always. The early church moved forward with prayer and fasting.

A Personal Call to Prayer

A persistent and prevailing prayer life is a primary proof that one is called by

God to minister. Prayer validates a person's claim to spiritual leadership. A leader or teacher who does not have a vital prayer life cannot be trusted in the things of God because spiritual truth is correctly comprehended only in loving communion with God through the Holy Spirit.

Carlo Carretto, in his book *The God Who Comes,* discussed how God's will becomes real to us in the practice of prayer and contemplation. He emphasizes how essential prayer is to the understanding of spiritual truth. Spiritual insight into God's true nature and workings is not humanly given. No one knows the things of God except by the Spirit of God. God and spiritual truth cannot be known through the intellect, through degrees or doctrines or theology alone but only when joined with prayer. "This is why," Carretto says, "I do not believe theologians who do not pray, who are not in humble communication of love with God."

Until we learn to pray, faith and spiritual power, yes, religious life as such, is a closed book. Where there is no effective prayer life, the very heart of spiritual life has ceased to beat, and our religious life becomes the deadness of form, custom, and dogma.

E. Stanley Jones wrote: "If I had one gift and only one gift to make to the Christian church, I would offer the gift of prayer. For everything follows from prayer.

Prayer tones up the total life. I've found that by actual experience I am better or worse as I pray more or less. If my prayer life sags, my whole life sags with it. If my prayer life goes up, my life as a whole goes up with it. To fail here is to fail all down the line; to succeed there is to succeed everywhere.

In true prayer the battle of the spiritual life is lost or won."[15]

Prayerless preachers or teachers or other spiritual leaders are not to be trusted to convey the truth of God. Without prayer, persons become stupid in spiritual things.

Is there any other thing which tests our obedience to the Scripture more than prayer? Is there anything that so tests our faith in God? Is there anything more commended and commanded than prayer? Especially leaders of God's people are to be persons of prayer. The great apostolic declaration is that "we will give ourselves to prayer and to the preaching of the Word" (Acts 6:4). Prayerless leaders are powerless leaders who produce prayerless and powerless followers. Until we learn to pray and know the revelation to spiritual truth which prayer brings, we remain unbelievers at heart regardless of how many doctrines we declare or how much theology we teach. Further, our work will not prosper and our people will stray.

Whenever there is a crisis in the church, it is always first a crisis of prayer.

Particularly for leaders one might question whether one has a call to ministry if one is not a person of prayer. It can be said for certain that a spiritual leader who is not a person of prayer is a leader living in disobedience to the repeated commands of Scripture to devote oneself to prayer.

Our influence for God finally depends upon our firsthand knowledge of the unseen world and our experience in prayer. Love, insight, and tact are born in prayer and contemplation. Hardness, spiritual blindness, and clashing with others result from lack of communion with God.

A certain preacher during the great Welsh revivals was marvelously success-ful. He had but one sermon, but through it hundreds were led to Christ.

Far away from the lonely valley where the faithful preacher lived, news of the wonderful success reached another preacher. He became eager to find out the secret of this ministry. He started out, and walked the long and dreary road, and at length, reached the humble cottage where the good minister lived.

"Friend," he asked, "where did you get your sermon?" He was taken into a poorly furnished room. The preacher pointed to a spot where the carpet was worn shabby and bare, near a window that faced the solemn mountains. The minister said, "Friend, that is where I got that sermon.

My heart was heavy for weeks. One evening I knelt there, and cried for power to preach as I never preached before. The hours passed until midnight struck, and the stars looked down on a sleeping valley and the silent hills; but the answer would not come. So I prayed on until at length I saw a faint gray shoot up in the East. Presently it became silver, and I watched and prayed until the silver became purple and gold and on all the mountain crest blazed the altar fires of the new day. Then the sermon came, and the power came, and I lay down and slept, and I arose and preached. And scores fell down before the fire of God. That is where I got my sermon!"

The Practice of Prayer

I would also seek to lead my congregation to become a praying congregation. Jesus said, "My house shall be called a house of prayer" (Matthew 21:13). I have come to believe that any congregation, with a tithe of its membership in daily intercession for the Lord's work, will prosper spiritually and in every way. So I would seek to lead my people in the practice of closet prayer, corporate prayer, covenant prayer, and constant prayer.

Jesus spoke about **closet prayer** when he said, "Whenever you pray, go into your room and shut the door and pray to your Father who is in secret; and your

Father who sees in secret will reward you" (Matthew 6:6).

God's urging to **corporate prayer** is scattered all through Scripture, illustrated again and again through history. God moves in a mighty way whenever God's people unite in prayer.

Covenant prayer carries great promise: "If two of you agree on earth about anything you ask, it will be done for you" (Matthew 18:19). The privilege and power of covenant prayer, whether of husband and wife or one believer with another, has been overlooked too much. But when it is grasped, and believers covenant together, the promises of God are fulfilled.

Constant prayer is the privilege of each believer wherever such may be. Then we can pray literally hundreds of times each day as we raise our voices in thanksgiving, praise, intercession, and petition. It is a wonderful thing to practice "constant prayer." And the minister who teaches people to pray will reap rich rewards in not only answered prayer but in changed lives and relationships. It is true that "prayer changes things" and "prayer changes persons."

No congregation will bear witness without united prayer, and no congregation will sustain persons who are led to Christ unless it is a praying congregation. Prayer prepares the people with compassion for others. Prayer prepares the hearts of those who need Christ.

≈ *IX* ≈

I would seek to always remember that my calling is not to control people's faith but to love them into the kingdom of God.

In Jeremiah 10:10-11 God complains because the shepherds have no compassion. Without compassion they become destroyers of God's vineyards.

It is very easy to lose a heart of compassion. *Compassion* is the word used most often in the New Testament to describe Jesus' feelings. People must sense our love for them if they are to respond to our ministry. They need to sense our "reaching-out" compassion in crisis, hurts, and longings.

There is a wonderful release and freedom in believing that God does the changing of lives. My work is not to change people. I am to love people and to accept people. It is the Holy Spirit's work to convince, convict, and convert. Oswald Chambers wrote: "Take care lest you play the hypocrite by spending all your time trying to get others right before you worship God yourself." A spiritual person will not demand that people believe this or that doctrine but that people conform their lives to the will and likeness of Christ.

It is a relief when the servant of Christ realizes that service is not to change persons or to control persons but to provide a relationship which frees persons to realize that freedom in Christ which delivers them from every prison and bondage. We are called by Christ to provide the contact and context in which Christ can give new life.

Early the minister is inclined to preach truth, as understood, regardless of whom or where it hits and hurts. With some spiritual maturity, the graces of patience, compassion, and mercy become more important. I have prayed many times, "Lord, let me speak the truth in love. If I cannot say it in love help me not to say it." Paul's greetings in the Epistles are "grace and peace." When writing to preachers, he writes "grace, *mercy,* and peace."

Loved into the Kingdom

If I make mistakes, I pray it will be on the side of mercy and love. Finally people are loved into the Kingdom and we will reach as many as we have the capacity of loving. "Love never fails."

In *The Voice from the Cross,* Andrew Blackwood shares a delightful story of how a preacher's love changed an entire community.

Two farm communities lie about five miles apart, under the same sun and clouds. The farmers in each district raise the same kinds of crops. They face the same problems year in and year out. Half of the people of one community are related to half of the people in the other. The two neighborhoods are as much alike as neighborhoods can be, in all but one important respect.

In one community there is strife. The fire department, the school board, and the grange are always scrapping back and forth. In the other community there is harmony, bearing of one another's burdens, pulling the load together.

The difference in the two communities can be traced to the influence of one man, a minister who lived in the friendly community for many years. He was no pulpit genius, nor was he a church organizer. But one thing he did constantly and well. He reflected the love of Christ. He loved people.

When he moved to the little church he found a congregation torn with dissension, in a neighborhood permeated with hatred. While he did not lack convictions, he loved both parties in every dispute and sought to guide them to a God-fearing solution. He loved people when they were detestable, and sometimes they were amazingly so. He looked for the good in the meanest of them, and he encouraged the good in the best of them. He lived to see a community transformed.

From an isolated church on the hilltop

where he labored in love, a constant stream of young men and women flowed in Christian vocations. Those who decided to stay at home lived like Christians.[16]

Perhaps it all seems like a little achievement, but consider what happens without love.

Years ago a brilliant and talented young leader was sent to the mission field. He was critical and controlling. He was quick-tempered and impatient. He rubbed people the wrong way and reacted against people.

Finally the people wrote to the mission board asking that he be called back since he was more of a hindrance than a help.

After the board met and discussed what should be done, the secretary wrote a letter to the young missionary. "You shall stay under one condition. The condition is that you read I Corinthians 13 each day for the next year." Before the year was half gone a transformation took place. The same persons who wrote asking for his dismissal now wrote asking for his continuance. In a few years the same persons wrote the board asking for him to become their bishop. And he served for more than fifty years as an effective leader of Christ's church.

Overflowing

True pastoral work is the outflowing of spontaneous love. Without love no skill in the world will help in the least; with love, no number of mistakes will make one fail. "Love never fails."

A young pastor began in a difficult spot in a large city. I stopped to see him. As we chatted in the city park he said, "I have covenanted with God that I will love every person God sends through those church doors." No wonder God is doing miracles of regeneration and people are coming to hear his message and to receive help from him.

At a large, interdenominational pastors' conference, a small group met for prayer between sessions. On the final day a pastor confessed that he had come to this conference to find help. If he did not find help he was leaving the ministry. "And God showed me here," he said, "that I do not love my people. I'm agitated and angry over their behavior.

God has shown me that I must, through the love of Christ, go back and love my people."

We joined in prayer, laying our hands on this pastor, asking God to fill him with divine love. Some months later I received a letter. "Things are really humming around here," he said. "God has given me a great love for my people."

Malcolm Muggeridge points out that the biggest disease today is not leprosy or tuberculosis but rather the feeling of being unwanted, uncared for, and deserted by everybody. And the greatest evil is the lack of love, the terrible indifference toward those who live by the roadside in need. For such we need to let the love of Christ flow through us.

≈ X ≈

I would seek to always be aware that God is at work, usually in persons, places, and programs where I least expect God to be working.

I have learned to more and more fear putting God in a box. Religious leaders of Jesus' day had God so figured out they could not see or understand his working right in front of them.

God is so refreshingly new that God seldom, if ever, does the same thing twice in the same way. Particularly, when I think I have God all figured out, he is working somewhere else and doing it in a different way than I had planned or expected. That is more and more exciting.

Oswald Chambers said, "When we are certain of the way God is going to work, he will never work in that way any more" (*My Utmost for His Highest*).

Italian theologian Carlo Carretto in *The God Who Comes* says, "If you ask me how God revealed himself to me I reply, 'He reveals himself in newness.' . . . God is eternally new. He never repeats himself."

One of the tests of spiritual sensitivity is the ability to see Christ at work, to hear his whisper above the words of the world and to sense his presence everywhere. Human nature waits and longs for the dramatic and the decided-upon method of how Christ works. The divine nature discerns his presence and work in solitude and silence, in the smallest happenings of each day, in the still small voice. It is to realize that God is already at work before I get there.

Fred B. Craddock in his book *Overhearing the Gospel* says that it is not our job to decide in advance who is good soil and to withhold the seed from all others. The gospel, if shared, will create and determine its own listeners. He tells of learning a lesson from an experience remembered from his shy and fearful adolescence. "A pretty girl had moved into our town and into our school. She was immediately popular. Admiring her from a distance, I asked her, in the privacy of my mind, to go with me to the movies. I looked at her, then looked at myself, and, in the privacy of my mind, she said no. For days afterward I was both hurt and angry at her rejection of me, a decision she was never allowed to make." So, says Craddock, "It may be that when we speak to many, only a few will hear, but we have not been called to speak to a few and then complain that there are not many."[17]

We ought always to pray and approach people with the thought that God is already at work in their minds and hearts. Christ died for each person, and knowing this we have God working in our favor already. The Holy Spirit is eager to make that Good News real to each person. So we have this urging in our favor, and sense God's Word will not return void. We also have this assurance to urge us to faithfulness.

Nor can we claim to be concerned for a lost world if we are not concerned for those whom we do meet day by day. If I were starting my ministry again I would remember that God is among his people. In "The Preacher's Mistake," Brewer Mattocks (a physician, author, and son of a Presbyterian minister) bumps us off our steeple.

The Parish Priest of Austerity
   climbed up in a high church steeple
To be nearer God,
   so that he might hand
   His word down to his people.

When the sun was high,
   when the sun was low,
The good man sat unheeding
   sublunary things
From transcendency
   was he forever reading.

And now and again,
   when he heard the creak
   of the weather vane turning,

He closed his eyes
  and said "Of a truth
  from God I now am learning."

And in sermon script
  he daily wrote
  what he thought was sent from heaven.
And he dropped this down

on his people's heads,
two times one day in seven.

In his Age God said—
  "Come down and die!"
And he cried out from the steeple,
  "Where art thou, Lord?"
And the Lord replied,
  "Down here among my people."[18]

≈ *XI* ≈

I would seek to always remember that I minister only out of overflow, and that fruit is produced only on new growth.

If I am barely making it myself I am giving little of worth to anyone else.

In his first epistle, the apostle John says that in Christ the Word was first audible: "We heard." Then it was visible—"We saw." The word became flesh. Finally it proved tangible—"We touched it with our hands." So in our ministry it is not simply to tell, to speak, or to preach the Word, as important as that is. People must also see that word in the life of the one who speaks. "The word must again become flesh." In addition that word must also prove true in the tangible, where we say ourselves, and others can say, "The truth was tested in the crucible of experience and life and it proved true."

Love, forgiveness, and all the truths of the gospel, must not only be proclaimed from the pulpit but they must be proclaimed and portrayed in the mundane, everyday relationships of life. Here is where the truth is tested. For this, there must be the development of the inner life or else what is said and done becomes hollow and hypocritical.

Effective ministry comes from those areas where I have allowed the Lord to touch me. Until God has performed his work in me, I will likely be more of a hindrance than a help to others in my ministry. This is not to say that God does not bless beyond my puny faith and weak endeavor. What it does say is that where I am most effective will be in the areas where God has called me to greater faithfulness, and where I have responded in obedience. I should not expect people to pray if I am not a person of prayer. I should not expect people to be sacrificial givers if I do not give sacrificially. I should not expect people to make fresh commitments if I am not an example. In all this the Scripture says a leader should be "an example of the believers."

A minister must be exhibit "A" of what he or she preaches and teaches. The message we preach must be modeled. Only as we are freed by Christ can we lead other persons to freedom in Christ. Only as we are released by Christ can we lead persons to release and only as we are growing can we lead persons to new growth. We should not expect our message to be effective if what we preach is not true in our lives. Henri Nouwen writes: "The great illusion of leadership is to think that a person can be led out of the desert by someone who has never been there."

President Eisenhower demonstrated the art of leadership with a simple piece of string. He put it on a table and said, "Pull it and it will go wherever you wish. Push it and it will go nowhere at all. It's just that way when it comes to leading people."

If I were beginning again, I would seek to be not only one who knows the way and shows the way, but also one who goes the way. The shepherd "goes before" the sheep.

Marks of False Leaders

In his last words within the temple walls, Jesus gave us three clear characteristics of false leaders. He called them hypocrites, blind guides, fools, and snakes.

That's strong language in Matthew 23, used to impress upon us Jesus' insight between false and true spiritual leaders.

1) False leaders are those who "do not practice what they preach." To ask people to be or do what we ourselves are unwilling to be or do is hypocritical. It is a mark of a false leader. Jesus says that such also place burdens on others, which they themselves will not bear. Beware of those who preach or teach what they do not practice. True spiritual leaders practice first, preach and teach second. True leaders say, "Follow me as I follow Christ." True leaders are those who not only know

and show the way but are also those who go that way.

2) False leaders are ostentatious. Jesus says, "Everything they do is done for people to see." Such leaders love a show. They do what will leave an impression for self, draw attention, and build one's own status and reputation. Such persons may have long prayers in public but short ones in private. They will give only if it is noticed. Uppermost is the desire to be seen. This attitude is a far cry from the ministry of those who sincerely say, "Not I but Christ be honored, loved, exalted."

3) False leaders love preeminence. Jesus says such "love the place of honor at banquets and the most important seats in the church." They love to be greeted in public places and to be called professor, doctor, president, reverend, and bishop. False leaders will be present when they are on center stage or in charge, but they seldom show up when someone else ministers or leads. False leaders love to be honored, lauded, and recognized for their position and attainments. "In honor preferring one another" is absent from their lives.

In contrast Jesus gives two tests of true spiritual leaders which continue current and clear. These are humility and servanthood. These are in such stark contrast to the marks of false leaders that they can be easily discerned. They will always characterize those who seek to serve and follow Christ.

Christ humbled himself and became a servant. True spiritual leaders will always be known by a spirit which turns people's eyes away from themselves to Christ. True leaders will seek the privilege to serve rather than a position to be served.

Fruit is produced on new growth, and all the fruit of the Holy Spirit is produced in relation to other people. We can only grow in long-suffering, for example, when one tests how long we can suffer; so for all the fruit. And God has always seemed to allow persons around who will test our love, patience, joy, and other fruit.

Over the years, in getting into many congregations, I have learned that each congregation has "a situation." After being with a congregation for several days, the pastor will usually share, "We have a 'situation' in this congregation." And that "situation" is usually a person who is making it hard for the pastor and others.

The test is whether I can continue to treat these, who confront and challenge me, with kindness, love, and respect. Others are waiting to see how a representative of Christ deals with difficult people. They know I love my friends, but they want to know if I can love those who oppose me—even my enemies—in the congregation. Here is where God teaches me the meaning of unanswered or unrequited love.

≈ XII ≈

I would be strongly drawn to church planting rather than to an established congregation.

I would ponder and pray much longer before deciding to become pastor of a congregation which has heard the gospel for years, which has many persons able to teach the Scripture, and which is filled already with many gifts and persons who vie, at times, for responsibility and position. Why not go where there is greater need?

While the established congregation is a challenge, and there is much need there, the established congregation is exactly that: "established." Usually, regardless of denomination, it is anti-growth and exclusive in spite of its talk otherwise. It is seldom, if ever, serious about evangelism. On its best days it is for the righteous and not for loving sinners.

I've learned that the most common expression in an established congregation when it begins to grow from the community is, "You'd never know this congregation anymore." Or, "This congregation used to be a nice little congregation without any problems." The implications of these statements are great. And these implications are soon felt by a newcomer. The established congregation can receive a very small percentage of newcomers—a few who marry into the right family or who keep fairly quiet in decision making. If this judgment is too harsh you will be glad for examples otherwise.

The established congregation, large or small, also does not produce the equivalent of its own pastoral leadership. Many times it has to go outside for its leaders.

While, without a doubt, the Lord calls pastors to minister to established congregations, if I were beginning my ministry again I'd feel a strong pull to church planting where there would be freedom and the excitement of reaching out to persons who have not repeatedly heard the gospel or for some reason are estranged from the established church.

I would try to keep in mind that a congregation will likely live with its original purpose. If a congregation is begun to meet the need of denominational members who move into an area, it will continue with that primary purpose and likely never be a church which reaches the community. If a congregation is begun with the primary purpose of reaching the needs and families of the community, it will continue to carry that perspective.

Therefore if I were starting my ministry again I would consider more carefully the need before deciding where to serve. If ten persons were carrying a heavy log and nine were at one end and one at the other, which end ought I to help? If one acre had only a few heads of wheat, while beside it a hundred acres were ripe for harvest, where ought I go to labor?

≈ *XIII* ≈

I would seek to be more disciplined in practicing the personal touch through visiting the flock.

In visitation hearts are opened and the gospel of Christ can be ministered in more personal ways. It is where the minister has a particular privilege to pray with and for persons in a personal way for all kinds of concerns and needs. It is true, a home-going pastor makes a church-going people. But, even more, a Christ-centered visitation program builds relationships to Christ and opens the hearts of persons more than any other one thing a minister can do. Visitation also builds a bond between pulpit and family. A people will not long hold to anything which is preached from the pulpit but not held to in the home.

A pastor who loves the sheep has to be with the sheep. Henry B. Williams advises, "I can learn more practical significance about the members of any given home by one pastoral call than I can gain in ten years by casually and hurriedly meeting these same people at the close of worship on Sunday morning."

In visitation more is learned than in a dozen seminars. Here we keep in contact with the questions people are asking. "The sermon always sounds better Sunday morning if I have had a shake of the pastor's hand during the week." Perhaps few can have the skill of the pastor who knew each of 5,000 members by name, but most can be much enriched through a program of visitation. It took me until my last pastorate before I had good feelings about my own practice of visitation, and even then I realized a much better job could be done. I wish I could begin again.

A Definite Plan

Because I do very little visitation without a definite schedule, I've found it helpful to have a plan to visit a certain group of persons each week, another group every two weeks, and some once a month. These categories will not be a large number of the congregation but include the shut-ins, the aged, and those with particular needs. Every member should be on the occasional list to be visited at least once a year. This is ministering the gospel "from house to house" (Acts 20:20).

A meaningful experience, which I would seek to do even more faithfully, is to make some contact at the school luncheon, or other setting, with every teen in the congregation. When I have done this, it has been most rewarding and has opened the door for youth to come to me later when a need of one kind or another arose.

I would always pray with and for my people when I visit them in the hospital or home. While there may be a circumstance or situation occasionally where it may be inappropriate to lead in prayer, this should surely be rare. People expect a minister to be a person of prayer and they expect the prayers of their spiritual leader. Time and again I have heard persons lament that the pastor visited them but did not have a prayer.

Chaucer in *The Canterbury Tales* gives a beautiful picture of a loving and visiting pastor.

The Word of Christ most truly did he preach,
And his parishioners devoutly teach.
Benign was he, in labors diligent,
As proved full oft . . .
Wide was his parish, scattered far asunder,
Yet none did he neglect, in rain, or thunder.
Sorrow and sickness were his kindly care;
With staff in hand he traveled everywhere.
This good example to his sheep he brought
That first he wrought, and afterward he taught.
This parable he joined the Word unto—
That "If gold rust what shall iron do?"
For if a priest be foul in whom we trust,
No wonder if a common man shall rust!

Though holy in himself and virtuous
He still to sinful men was piteous,
Not sparing in his speech, in vain
    conceit,
But in his teaching kindly and discreet.
He drew his flock to heaven with noble
    art,
By good example, was his holy art.
No less did he rebuke the obstinate,
Whether they were of high or low
    estate.
For pomp and worldly show he did not
    care;
No morbid conscience made his rule
    severe.
The lore of Christ and his apostles
    twelve
He taught, but first he followed it him-
    self.[19]

Particularly New Persons

Yes, if I were starting my ministry again
I would seek to help myself and my members be aware of new persons moving into
our communities. If approximately one
fourth of the population moves each year,
particularly in the more urban areas, then
a vast opportunity for new contacts is always present.

My most successful outreach over the
forty years of my ministry has been in
contacting new persons and families who
move into the area. If such say they are a
part of another denomination, I called the
pastor of that denomination and told the
pastor of such new persons in the area. If
they had no church home I would return

to my study, write a letter of welcome to our community and to the congregation with information about the congregation, its history, activities, and opportunities. I would also make families of my congregation aware of such new persons and encourage contacts for such. Families need to catch the vision and have some training in how to meet newcomers.

≈ *XIV* ≈

I would beware of particular pitfalls in the ministry.

As a young pastor, I was greatly helped by an aged minister who shared with me that, when there is spiritual shipwreck, the cause usually is one of three areas. These three are brought together in Hebrews 12:14-16. Here are three barriers to blessedness, usefulness, and happiness. Understanding these will protect our own ministry and also enable us to help others.

First is the *barrier of bitterness.* "See to it that no one misses the grace of God and that no bitter root grows up to cause trouble and defile many" (12:14 NIV).

Bitterness is an attitude toward another which begins in the heart. It is a root buried beneath the surface so that it cannot be seen at first. But it stops the stream of spiritual blessedness. It hinders prayer. It stifles our message. It grieves the Holy Spirit. Bitterness finally defiles many others.

Here we see the seriousness of allowing even a root of bitterness within. Not only does it rob the bitter person of spiritual blessing and make God distant but it also destroys relationships in the family, the church, and beyond.

Therefore the appeal of Scripture is that we should not fail to receive the grace of God, which is God's undeserving love for us. In turn we are to treat others just like God treats us and not be bitter toward anyone. Beware of the root of bitterness.

Second is the *barrier of behavior.* See to it "that no one is sexually immoral" (12:16 NIV). We must be on guard against any kind of immorality, first in thought and also in act.

No one is a sudden moral failure. Lust like bitterness is allowed to lodge in the heart and mind. Immorality is a barrier to beholding the face of God. "The pure in heart see God." The impure also develop wrong concepts about God, about sin, and about others.

I have found that when there is hidden moral sin, persons are inclined to move in one of two directions. One is to become very libertine and take a light view of sin. The other is to become very legalistic, rigid, and unforgiving, taking a hard and judgmental attitude toward others.

Satan is subtle and seeks to destroy the most effective servants of Christ by leading them, little by little, into lustful thoughts and then into lustful behavior. And we cannot be too careful in our thought life and relationships. We need to ask for God's hedge of protection, lest we fall to the enticements and seductions which will surely come in our ministry. Through lustful trickery the devil has destroyed the effectiveness of many a minister. Through immorality the devil has slain many a servant of God.

I respect the ministers who want a window in their study door and who will not counsel the opposite sex alone in a building. And I believe that I, as a minister, must continually remind myself of God's standard of purity and fidelity, for impurity is surely one of the great pitfalls of the pastor.

The third pitfall is the *barrier of belongings.* See to it that no one "is godless like Esau, who for a single meal sold his inheritance right as the oldest son. Afterward, as you know, when he wanted to inherit the blessing, he was rejected. He could bring about no change of mind, though he sought the blessing with tears" (12:16-17 NIV).

Esau became the example in all ages of one who sells out the spiritual for the material, who valued his stomach above his soul, and who majored in real estate rather than relationships. Yes, we as ministers need the great warning and great promise of Hebrews 13:5: "Put greed out of your lives and be content with such things as you have. God himself has said, I will never leave you or forsake you."

I have known ministers over the years who never settled this one, and they were forever unhappy. Their service was ineffective. They became envious of others and became complaining of their own salary and situation.

Envy and greed are the temptations not only of the rich but also of the poor. These sins, warned against so often in the Scrip-ture, can be a barrier to God's blessing in our lives and a barrier in one's ministry to others.

If I were beginning my ministry again I would commit myself not to let these attitudes ever linger in my life. These three are particular pitfalls for the person in a spiritual ministry.

≈ *Additional Timeless Wisdom* ≈

I would commit myself to never say anything from the pulpit which I am unwilling to speak to a person about individually. In other words, the pulpit is not the place for a personal attack.

Early in my ministry a person called me to task for what he thought was a personal attack in my preaching. I assured him that I did not have him or any other one person in mind. I shared with him the above commitment and asked him if he felt I'd kept it. He replied that he felt I had done so, and the rift was healed.

❧

I would seek to always keep a confidence. Many a minister has lost effectiveness, not because of lack of ability but because the minister betrayed a confidence.

❧

I would seek to remember not to get off the train when I'm going through the tunnel. There are plenty of discouragements in ministry, but it is not good to make a major decision during times of discouragement. Usually, in the first three years of ministry, as in marriage, we have a period of disillusionment. That is not the time to make a sudden move. It is especially wise to get the counsel of a number of spiritual, discerning persons at such a time and not to listen to one or two who tend to see only the negative side of things.

❧

I would seek to remember that the most successful leader is not the one who knows or does everything but the one who knows his or her strengths and weaknesses and who has the ability to find those who are strong in areas where he or she is weak and empower such.

❧

I would pray for just enough encouragement to keep going strong for God. God seldom, if ever, allows his servants to see how great a blessing they are. He allows just enough encouragement to make us fruitful, but even the fruit is not for the benefit of the preacher but for the refreshment of others.

I would beware of letting compliments build self-confidence in spiritual things. The compliments of others can be used for evil if we are not determined to give all glory to God. The more gifted, the greater the temptation and thirst for praise. As we grow older the craving for praise leads to frustration and bitterness, followed by contrived efforts to get attention and affirmation.

≈

I would seek to remember that, regardless how hard a person appears, each one has an inlet. If I row around long enough I will find the inlet and be able to reach the person for Christ who died for this person as much as for any other.

≈

I would remember that Jesus changed people by love, acceptance, and forgiveness. The Pharisees tried to change people by criticism, judgment, and condemnation.

≈

I would seek to remember that Jesus did not spend time or effort justifying or vindicating himself. St. Augustine prayed, "O Lord, deliver me from the lust of vindicating myself." A great pitfall of many a leader is to seek vindication, to explain oneself, to excuse failure, and to put oneself in a good light. Jesus did none of it.

The lust for vindication is the lust for approval. Oswald Chambers wrote: "Our insistence in proving that we are right is nearly always an indication that there has been some point of disobedience."

Therefore, I would seek to let the Lord fight my battles for me as he promised. When I seek to fight my own battles the Lord steps aside and lets me fight alone. When I step aside he will do the vindicating and work all things for his glory and my good.

It was said of one preacher, "If you want to feel his love, hurt him." He had such divine love that it overflowed especially in the midst of opposition, ill-will, and personal injury.

❧

I would seek to keep myself free from the love and lust for the material. Some ministers I have known became unhappy and even left the ministry entirely because they became discontented with their income, and left the spirit of sacrifice and service out of the desire for the material. A minister will be forever unhappy and unproductive spiritually who allows the spirit of discontent or greed to begin to grow.

❧

I would seek out several spiritual, wise, and sound counselors who have the concern for the church and my well-being in their hearts, to whom to go for counsel and perspective. Such can save from many a pitfall and wrong or skewed perspective, which a minister can easily develop or which can be developed through the compliments or criticisms of one or two other persons.

This means also, I would not take the adverse reaction of one person too seriously without checking such criticism with other trusted leaders who can advise with candor and love. I have suffered most in ministry for allowing broad, sweeping criticism from one person, who claimed to be speaking for many, only to discover it was a very personal reaction, backed only by some personal prejudice or agenda, and not the opinion of others at all.

❧

I would gather around me a few persons deeply committed to daily prayer and fasting for the church and for its ministry. To pray is to join the saints of all the ages and to join with Christ the great High Priest and intercessor in his concern for the whole world. The ministry of the Holy Spirit is linked with prayer more than any other aspect of the Spirit's ministry.

I have come to believe that a minister should not seek to minister without a group of prayer partners who will hold the minister before the throne of grace for divine preservation, proclamation, and empowerment.

❧

I would avoid envy like the plague. Envy is to feel sad when another is glad. It raises its ugly head when someone succeeds in the area I work or in the area I seek to be successful. Envy makes bitter persons and puts one in competition with another. Envy arises out of the basic evil of pride.

Oscar Wilde, in one of his stories, discusses how the devil was crossing the Libyan Desert when he met a number of his associates tempting a holy hermit. They tried to tempt the hermit with sins of the flesh, tempting him in every way they knew, but to no avail. The saint was steadfast and shook off all suggestions. Finally after watching their failure, in disgust the devil whispered to the tempters, "What you do is too crude. Permit me one moment." Then the devil whispered to the holy man, "Your brother has just been made a Bishop in Alexandria." A scowl of jealousy crossed the serene face of the hermit. "That," said Satan to his subordinates, "is the sort of thing I recommend."

❧

One of the subtleties of leadership and preaching is to think that by preparing a word of the Lord for my people I myself am therefore faithful and obedient. I would be on particular guard so that the truth I preach and teach is that which I myself first surrendered to and experience.

❧

I would remember that my love for Christ and the church is revealed as genuine when I can sincerely rejoice over the success and achievements of my successor and in the success of other ministers in congregations.

&

I would seek to keep in mind that, when my ministry is finished, I will have very likely influenced people more as a person than as a preacher. The final test is not how gifted I am but how godly I have lived. Will Garrison wrote: "In the only judgment that matters we will be measured not so much by what we have done as by what we have become."

&

I would ask God to deal with pride of any kind and to give me a spirit of Christlike humility. C. S. Lewis points out that the essential vice, the utmost evil, is pride. All sins of the flesh are flea bites in comparison. "Pride is essentially competitive."

He suggests, "If you want to find out how proud you are, the easiest way is to ask yourself, 'How do I dislike it when other people snub me, or refuse to take any notice of me, or shove their oar in me, or patronize me, or show off?'"

Lewis also points out that pride or self-conceit is the sin we are most conscious of in others and which we are most blind to in ourselves. The more we have it ourselves the more we dislike it in others. The opposite virtue is humility. Pride takes delight in shining or seeking to set others straight. It is out of pride we criticize and judge others. Humility is the most conscious of one's own failure and need of God's continual grace.

❧

I would seek to give my family the proper place. The order of priority is God, family, work. And this includes the preacher's family. For any one of these to get out of this order means all three relationships will suffer. Surely there are those times, as in everyone's experience, when the family must take a back seat. But, at the very best, my family should have the same claim on my time that the members of my congregation have. Hopefully, my family should have special claim on my time, love, attention, patience, and care. Here is also where I need to practice what I preach. For what should it profit me to gain a great pastorate and lose my own family? "If anyone does not know how to manage his own family, how can he take care of God's church?" (I Timothy 3:5 NIV).

❧

I would seek to accept the limits of my humanity. I will never be able to do all that needs to be done. I cannot meet the need of every person. I cannot be in peak performance in every board meeting, in every sermon, and in every meeting, and in meeting every need which presents itself. Some things will be left undone.

My concern should be not my human frailty but rather to avoid a spirit of laziness, indifference, negligence, or procrastination. God will take up the slack of my frailty, but I must develop the discipline of faithfulness and diligence.

&

I would remember that some of the areas of life where I've been helped most as a person and pastor were those in which some layperson questioned my thinking or approach. Without this challenge we forget our fallibility. To look at the layperson's doubt or questions will save me, in the end, from playing God and from pontificating. I would pay particular attention to the lowly, because God gives special insight and wisdom to such individuals.

&

If I were a minister again I'd do all I could to promote strong Christ-centered families, beginning with a carefully prescribed premarital counseling program and continue guidance to the newly married, young parents, middle-aged, aged, and singles. In other words, I would seek to provide continuous help to all the family. A congregation can be no more spiritual than its families, and if families are not making it, it becomes hard to hear what God is saying in other areas of life.

&

I would seek to remember that any group of leaders needs both the optimist and the pessimist. Prime Minister, Lord Asquith said, "It's an excellent thing to have an optimist at the front providing there is a pessimist at the rear." Jesus had a Peter who jumped into things quickly and a Thomas who questioned.

Pastors need to be optimists with spurs. I have never known a successful pastor who was a pessimist. Yet, I admit, pessimists in my congregations were a real irritation until I realized that such persons many times saved me from premature action. I may have had the spurs, but those who held the reins also caused me to think through an idea a second time.

ঽ

I would do more reading. I've never known an effective preacher or teacher who was not also a great lover of books. For those who minister there must be the constant reading of the inexhaustible Scriptures. John Wesley insisted that his preachers and assistants should be read-

ers. "Steadily spend all morning in this employ," he writes, "or at least five hours in the twenty four."

One Methodist historian credits Wesley with the publication of 371 works— this from the preacher who traveled more miles and who preached more sermons than any other man has ever done.

ঽ

I would seek to spread the joy of the Lord. The word of the gospel is "Good News" and it gives "eternal hope and good encouragement. The joy of the Lord is your strength."

Ministers live so much with people's problems, with cancer and heart attacks, with alcoholism and depression, in funeral homes and in hospitals, that it is possible to begin to live in darkness and gloom. Ministers are drawn to people who are hurting.

While the Christian message and mission dare not gloss over or dodge the sorrow, suffering, and gloom, neither dare it center here. The light of Christ and the resurrection penetrate the darkness and give glorious hope and joy to all who put faith in Jesus Christ.

≈ *Endnotes* ≈

1. William Nelson. *Ministry Formation for Effective Leadership* (Abingdon, 1988), p. 23.
2. James N. McCutcheon. *The Pastoral Ministry* (Abingdon, 1978), p. 12.
3. David J. Bosch. *A Spirituality of the Road* (Herald Press, 1979), p. 13.
4. G. Byron Deshler. *For Preachers Only* (Zondervan, 1973), unpaginated.
5. Dallas Willard. *The Spirit of the Disciplines* (Harper & Row, 1988), p. 166.
6. Thomas R. Swears. *The Approaching Sabbath* (Abingdon, 1991), p. 86.
7. Suzanne Johnson. *The Christian Spiritual Formation in the Church and Classroom* (Abingdon, 1991), p. 69.
8. Dwight L. Grubbs. *Beginnings—Spiritual Formation for Leaders* (Fairway Press), p. 56.
9. E. Stanley Jones. *The Christ of the Mount* (Abingdon, 1931), pp. 13-14.

10. Eldon Trueblood. *Signs of Hope* (Harper & Row, 1950), p. 122.
11. Henri Nouwen. *Making All Things New* (Harper & Row, 1981), pp. 79-80.
12. Carlo Carretto. *The God Who Comes* (Orbis Books, 1974), pp. 183-184.
13. Elizabeth O'Connor. *Called to Commitment* (Harper & Row, 1963), p. 94.
14. Bill Hull. *The Disciple-Making Pastor* (Fleming H. Revell, 1988), p. 15.
15. E. Stanley Jones. *How to Pray* (Abingdon, 1943), p. 3.
16. Andrew Blackwood. *The Voice from the Cross* (Baker House, 1955), pp. 63-64.
17. Fred B. Craddock. *Overhearing the Gospel* (Abingdon, 1978), p. 39.
18. William A. Armstrong. *Minister, Heal Thyself* (Pilgrim Press, 1985), pp. 21-22.
19. Chaucer. *The Canterbury Tales*, "Prologue" (_. _. Leonard).